This book is dedicated to my sons and daughters graduating from college as they enter into Corporate America Dwayna, Wilbert Jr., Christopher, and Tanisha

10 Rules For

Minorities Entering Corporate America

Or

10 rules for African-Americans, Latinos, Women, Asians, Native Americans and other minorities entering corporate America.

10 Rules for Minorities Entering Corporate America

VMS Publishings & Productions, Inc.

Publishing Dept

Post Office Box 442

Conley, Ga. 30288

Edition ISBNs   978-0-9820080-2-7

Library of Congress Control Number: 2012922390

Library of Congress Subject Headings:

African Americans -- Employment.

 Minorities -- Vocational guidance -- United States.

 Career development -- United States.

  Success in business.

First Edition 2014

Second Edition 2018

Cover Photography by Christopher Allen Richardson

Push_director@yahoo.com

Proof read by B.J. Cleveland

2.0

The 10 Rules

Preface-Note to the Reader

This book is intended to help you start creating your unique personal brand for your career and your life. Branding is the intentional act of standing out from the crowd and clearly defining who you are and what you represent. This helps others to think of you for a job position, project or even a business venture because they know what you stand for and what you do well. Your personal brand is with you 24/7, taking it with you everywhere you go, to everyone you meet. Your brand should exude through every facet of your life, personal and professional. As you go through this book, start thinking about who you are and what you represent. Let this book jump start that process. Write down your thoughts on your unique personal brand and other rules to help enhance your personal brand in the space provided at the end of this book.

Number 1 Rule: CYA–Cover Your "As_the_world_turn"

The number one rule for any new job or new position you attain in Corporate America is always CYA. To do this you must document any and everything you do in an easily accessible method, preferably in a digital format. Treat every request received from a user, peer and manager as a traceable document that is filed in a manner in which you can easily access and remember its location. Derive a personal filing system to file every e-mail, document and requests relevant to your projects, job, and department. It is not necessary to save every e-mail coming to your inbox because every e-mail will not relate specifically to your work. But any work requested of you, no matter how small the task must be documented for your protection, your group's protection, and even your manager's protection.

Here is an example; a user approaches you in the hallway and asks you to change a title on a report. This is a small task, so you inform him or her that you will implement that small change. During the conversation, tell the user to send you an e-mail and copy your manager about the small request. If the user does not send the e-mail request in a timely manner but still needs the small change; execute the changes on the report and kindly send an e-mail copying your manager with a message stating, according to our discussion on "such and such" date your requested changes have been completed. Below is an example of an e-mail whereby you completed a small change request to a report but the user does not send you a formal request---

From: VSingleton@VMSPublishing.com
To: UserName@VMSPublishing.com
CC: MyManager@VMSPublishing.com
UserName,
According to our discussion on 12/22/2013, your request to change the header "'ACCT" to "Account Number" has been completed. Attached is a copy of the report. Please let me

know if you need further clarification or if you have any questions concerning this request.

Thanks...
V. M. Singleton
Lead Marketing Database Manager
...and do have a nice day!!!

This email documents your work, when the work was completed, who requested the change and demonstrates your collaborative spirit.

For every project that you are responsible for, you need to develop a system to track

- ➢ Who requested it,

- ➢ What was requested,

- ➢ When the request was processed and

- ➢ Documents a history of the original request from the user and the deliverable (ex. File, database or reports).

Most of the time your department will have in place a request for change process for users and usually you or someone in your group can input small requests. First check your department's policy for inputting user requests for small or cosmetic changes. Sometimes a user will give an oral request. No matter how small, insignificant or cosmetic a change is, you must keep track of it. If the project is a recurring daily, weekly or monthly process, create an internal request procedure within the project to track the original source data and the deliverable sent to the user. If your job pertains to another profession like logistics, project lead or engineer, research a way to audit your requests, inputs, and deliverables. Consequently if anyone questions their requests or your deliverables, you have a backup system to investigate any concerns.

Also decide how long to keep digital backups or other audits. Eventually you will have a storage space issue and two to five years of backups should suffice but check with your company about retention of backup files.

Networking Is Essential

Networking has been one of the hardest things for me to put into effect. But it is the second most important rule to implement if you want to be successful in your career in corporate America. At one of my jobs I was told by my General Manager that this is a developmental area for me. It was a part of my annual review that I had to demonstrate I was putting forward an effort.

So this is how I started and so far it has been successful for me. I sent meeting invites once a month to General Managers, Directors and Vice Presidents for a 30-minute coffee break in the cafeteria between 8 and 9:30 am to people that I had a relationship with.

My conversation would be centered on what I did in the company and the value that I can bring to his or her department. I would in turn ask them what their department does and what advice they can give me for my career at this company to get the conversation started. If they gave me advice on others to network with then I would send invites out stating that "so and so manager name" thought you would be a good person to talk to. And that is how I expanded my network.

Most people will accept your invites. Don't be nervous, just be you and keep the conversation casual, informative and comfortable. Your goal is to interact with others, discuss what value you bring to him or her, exchange information, and develop contacts that will further your career. After each network meeting, I would follow up with a "thanks for meeting with me" email.

The more you network, the more it will be easier to ascend to your next position. It is not so much what you know that will get your career moving forward, it is who you know. Trust and Believe...it is 40% of your skills and 60% of who you know.

Start Each Job on the Ground Running

As soon as you have accepted the job offer, cleared your drug test along with the background check, research how long it takes to get to work to the new job location during regular business hours. Once you know what the drive time is, plan to be to work on your first day exceptionally early, and preferably before traffic starts in your area. On the first day, your goal is to get to your job 30 minutes early.

For one of my jobs in 2012, I took a test drive to my new job without traffic, it took me 22 minutes. My first day at my new job in traffic I left one hour and a half and it took me one hour and twenty minutes to the parking garage. I was praying to God that I would find the building, remember my manager's name and not be too late. I would rather be 30 minutes early to prepare myself, check my paperwork and get ready to greet my new manager.

For your first day at work, dress one level above the required dress code at your workplace which will help establish your unique personal brand. If the company's dress code is casual, your dress code is business casual and so on. Most of the time coworkers and managers do not see us so I use this one artifice to set myself above the rest to help managers and others see me and then appreciate my work. If you're seriously ambitious, dress for your next position that you have already determined in your career path. If you are a manager, dress as a manager, even if you are working at a manufacturing plant and most of your time is spent on the floor with the crew. You do not want upper management to mistake you for the crew. You are the manager, and you want upper management to distinguish easily you from the crew when they visit the plant. Of course, if the dress code is business suits you should maintain that dress code. As time progresses you will acclimate yourself to the dress code for that environment.

On your first day you probably will be led around to meet everyone, your manager will give you an overview about what the actual job entails and how the culture is at your new job environment. Take it all in, listen intently, look him or her in the eyes and ask pertinent questions about the work. You probably will not have anything to work on for a week or two, so bring something that will be useful for your job, like an iPad, cell phone, pen, and pad. Also bring all pertinent documents: your social security card, valid driver's license, passport, digital photo of yourself to obtain an id badge, completed I-9 forms and any other information your job has requested. These items will help keep you busy on your first day after orientation because your manager probably will be busy trying to get your information and equipment ordered and set up. Here's a list of other suggested to-do items:

➢ Attend orientation or view orientation video

➢ Familiarize yourself with the building (bathrooms, break rooms, cafeteria, gym room, etc)

➢ Bring extra cell phone charger

➢ Bring professional books to office to peruse during your downtime

Request company User ID

Request a company access badge

Review and enroll in medical benefits

Review and enroll in 401k plan

If applicable, transfer previous company 401k to current company 401k or a separate individual retirement fund

Check into business discounts offered by the company

Review other company perks offered

After all the introductions, be sure to obtain a couple of cell numbers from your coworkers so you can get back into the building until you receive your official security entry badge. Also check if your company issues temporary badges. Every company has security so you will have to be careful not to get locked out of the building your first couple of weeks and not be able to contact no one in the office. I know the first couple of weeks will be mind-numbing so do not bring anything personal to do while you twiddle your thumbs waiting for the real work to begin. Remember we are measured by a different stick; it's not fair, it's not intentional; it's just corporate America. It is what it is, so deal with it.

The first week on the job is critical. Your first week's agenda is to get familiar with the landscape. Meaning, in addition to getting to know where the bathroom, pencils and paper are located, you need to get familiar with the following:

➤ Familiarize yourself with the department's standards, processes, and procedures.

➤ Locate the department's main source for storing data, programs, spreadsheets or whatever is the main deliverable in your department.

➤ Research what is the mode of operation for receiving requests in the department , who assigns work to you, what are your main deliverables, who are your users, and what are the usual Service Level Agreements (SLA) or due dates to deliver completed work.

Your goal is to do all you can upfront to prepare for you first assignment so you can hit the ground running.

Usually your manager assigns work to you but there are times when you are assigned to a project and the manager delegates this task to the project manager, therefore he or she would be the person assigning work to you. After receiving your user-id and password, start checking accesses you need to all necessary files, tools and systems in order to do your job. If there are others already in the group, locate a coworker you can model your profile after for access to the department's files, data systems, and deliverables.

Finally it is mandatory that you come into work before time or on time especially for the next three months. You need to demonstrate you are dependable and you stand out from the rest of the crowd. In other words, start your unique personal brand. This mindset should also be applied to moving to a new department or a new position within the company.

Complete Your Projects Before or On Time

SLA's (Service Level Agreements) or due dates are necessities on projects to ensure that managers prioritize and complete work in a timely manner. You need to know what part of the project is your responsibility, and it is your first priority to complete your tasks before passing the project onto the next coworker or the end user. The last thing you want to be perceived as is the weak link in the chain. Your goal is to be either one of the strongest on the team or at least the subject matter expert for some part of the project; remember you are establishing your unique brand. Once you have received a due date for your project tasks, calculate your own personal SLA or due date for your work two to five days ahead of schedule if possible. Completing your work early provides you time to clean up any unforeseen errors and is very impressive to managers to deliver before a due date. If you are not able to complete the work before time, at least complete the work on time.

After sending your completed work, confirm that the user has received the requested information, data files, spreadsheets, tables, reports etc... For example, when you are assigned a project or task, ensure you understand the requirements and deliverables in the planning meetings. The planning meeting is where all parties on the project meet to determine the tasks, who are assigned to each task and the due date of each task. Take notes in this meeting to record each task discussed. Below is an example of what you need to capture in this meeting:

Task	Assigned To	Deliverable	Due Date
Add zip to report	B. Cleveland	Zip Test File	10-Jul
Correct Report Heading	V, Singleton	June Report	15-Jul

After the tasks have been assigned, the project leader usually sends out an email with a Business Requirement Document and project plan detailing the assignments and the due dates to all team members on the project.

Sometimes if this is a small request, no one sends out the project requirements and project plan but fortunately since you took notes you can volunteer to email this information out to everyone. Send the e-mail to the requestor with a synopsis of the deliverable requested, copying your manager or project lead and others who attended the planning meeting using the template example shown earlier in the chapter.

Do not forget your first priority and that is to complete the work assigned to you before or on the due date. Once you have completed the project, send the deliverable and copy all relevant parties, including your manager or project lead, stating you have completed your tasks assigned.

Here's a situation I encountered with a project I worked on. I had to complete tasks with the deliverable being a data file to another programmer working in another department. The second programmer performed additional calculations on my file and sent the data to the call center where a customer service representative would use the final data to help customers. After I completed my part of the project, I sent an e-mail to my manager, the second programmer, the second programmer's manager, the customer service representative and the customer service's manager. The second programmer completed his tasks and informed me earlier that week he would have the final data out the next day so everything would be in place and ready for use. On the next day, I confirmed with the second programmer that he had received my file and it was picked up by the downstream process. I contacted the customer service representative to review the new data on her screen. As fate would have it, the customer service representative did not see the new data on her screen. I proceeded to get all parties involved on a conference call to figure out at what point the data did not get processed. Of course, we did find that the second programmer did not check that the customer service representative received her deliverable.

So my first point is that my data file was not due to the end user (the customer service representative) but to a second programmer. Even though I had verified that I had completed my part successfully, my job is not complete until the final product gets to the end user. My second point is it is not my job to check if the second programmer completed his work successfully, but it is my practice to go a step farther to ensure the delivery of the final product whenever possible. Of course, I scored kudos for going that extra mile, which strengthens my personal brand to everyone involved on that project.

If you are fortunate enough to lead a project, create a Plan A for completing the project. While in the research phase of the project always document your risks and have alternate Plan B and Plan C for obstacles you foresee that might be a problem. If all "H_E_Double_Hockey_Sticks" break lose you at least have alternate plans. If all your planning fails, ensure you have done all that you can do to get the project back on track; and make sure while you were trying to complete the project on time that you did the Number 1 Rule-CYA.

Always document every phase of your project and keep your manager in the loop on major milestones and escalations. Some helpful procedures to put in place when leading a project are:

- ➤ Always get the requestor to sign off on the requirements document agreed upon in the requirements meeting

- ➤ Create an internal Project Development Plan for your team (I use MS Project)

- ➤ Create a test plan to systematically test all possible scenarios for each process that is changing

- ➤ Schedule a weekly status meeting and as you get closer to the project deadline schedule daily status meetings

- ➤ Backup process, data and reports before the project changes begin. Assure that all normal processes and procedures continue to run

- Create a separate directory to perform new changes to processes

- Peer Review and test each major change separately before implementing changes permanently

- If more than one process is changing, perform a system wide test to assure all new and old processes are working as expected

- If possible parallel test the new process versus the old process to validate the new data or new reports. Record, research and resolve any unexpected results

- Create a log to track problems, concerns, issues and resolutions

- Create a User Test Plan

- Once the changes are complete, send the deliverables to the user to test and approve before implementing the changes or new process

➤ After the changes are implemented, meet with your internal team to go over lessons learned and what you could have done better.

5

Triage Your E-mails

The e-mail application is the number one communication tool companies' use; therefore it is a key factor to supporting the Number 1 Rule-CYA. You need to develop a system to archive your e-mails with the e-mail thread to your personal folders. My recommendation is to set a monthly calendar reminder to perform your archive process at the beginning of the month for last month's e-mails. When your sent e-mail box is full, archive the e-mails to your hard drive, company-share folder or a memory stick. This practice is for the Number 1 Rule-CYA so when users or other colleagues come back months later inquiring about reports or stating you did not deliver requested documents in a timely manner, you have documentation. The most important factor of the e-mail system is that it is documented communication between you and others within and outside the company.

Whenever you receive an e-mail, especially concerning a project, file your e-mail in the appropriate Personal e-mail folder in a timely manner for that project. Keep in mind if you save your e-mails to your computer, the probability of your computer crashing will result in losing your archived e-mails. So my recommendation is to use the company's share-drive as they backup and maintain all information.

One more detail I would like to make concerning emails. The first thing I do when I get to work and logon to my computer every morning is open my emails. Next, I click to sort my emails by from and look for my manager's emails first. Since I received hundreds of emails a day I want to make sure I address my manager's concerns first and even my manager's manager emails as well. The last thing you want is for your manager to think his or her concerns are not your concerns.

6

Separate Business from Personal

E-mails from friends, accessing sexual explicit websites or any unauthorized websites according to your company's policy should be done privately on your own personal time and personal equipment. Do not engage in any such behavior on your company's property or business laptop. Remember, everything in this electronic age produces an electronic footprint so be mindful of what you do on the company's computer, electronic devices including the company-owned cell phone. Listed below are actions if not followed can lead to job termination:

➢ Do Not access sexual elicit websites EVER.

➢ Do Not access any unauthorized websites.

➢ Do Not access social media.

➢ Do Not send and receive e-mails from your friends or family.

- Do Not make too many personal phone calls while on the job.

- Do Not spend too much time visiting your friends at his or her cubicle or even your cubicle.

- Do Not send or receive personal faxes.

- Do Not take days off unless authorized by your manager.

- Do Not take office supplies for any reason.

- Do Not mention or misrepresent your company on your personal Social Media websites at no time unless authorized by your company.

My personal rule is race, religion, and politics do not belong in the work place. People have varying strong opinions and in corporate America there is no need to cause unnecessary strife within the work place. Race, sexism and sexual orientation are particularly sensitive subjects especially in the workplace so please refer to your company policy in regards to this subject matter.

There will be a situation when someone says or does something that is inappropriate. This you cannot avoid but you can take action and respond. My rule of thumb is if someone says or does something inappropriate then you need to nip it in the bud immediately; even standing there and saying nothing still signifies to anyone it is ok to say or do this inappropriate thing. So here is what I do: either I have a quick snap back so he or she knows not to say that again or I need to pull that person aside to let him or her know that it was inappropriate and it needs to stop. If the above does not work then my next step is to go to management. Hopefully your manager addresses the situation but if not then your next option is to go to Human Resources which should prompt an investigation. I have never escalated any of my concerns to Human Resources so I am not sure about the procedures but one of the functions of that department is to protect your civil rights.

My one advice is do not ever joke along with racist or sexist remarks because it gives him or her permission to take the behavior to another level. You have to address the remarks head on or the situation will continue to get more absurd each time you encounter that person.

7

Manage Your Manager

One of your top priorities is to ensure your manager look good by delivering exceptional work. Your second priority is to manage your manager by reassuring him or her that the best decision he or she made was to hire you. Here are some examples and situations I have implemented:

➢ While working overtime or on weekends to make a dead line, send a status report during off hours not only to keep him or her informed but also to give your manager a clue about the level of effort you are putting in to complete your assignments.

➢ For any systems or processes you support, become the Subject Matter Expert (SME) and put forth effort to have an overall understanding of downstream and upstream processes.

When obvious processes, procedures or documentation is missing within the group, be the one to point it out and present a solution.

When the opportunity presents itself volunteer for critical projects so when layoffs come (and they will come) and your manager has to downsize his or her department, your name will be the last one on his or her list because of your work ethic. Similarly when an opportunity arises you will be the first person he or she engages.

When you have one-on-one time with your manager, ask questions about his or her concerns and how can you bring more value to the department.

Find out what gaps he or she feels is missing from processes and procedures. Gather this information, create solutions and when appropriate present your solutions to the concerns the two of you discussed.

By keeping him or her pleased with your work ethic, how you complete projects before or on time and how you think outside of the box to help him or her solve the department's issues, you will begin to build favor and your personal brand with your manager. This will build a good rapport with your manager who will in turn become an advocate for you to other managers, promotions and critical projects.

8

Invest In Company 401K

Investing in a 401K plan is a company benefit I had never heard of when I landed my first job and I had no help from my family because they did not know about 401k plans. If you have a 401K plan at your new job, this is an opportunity for you to save a little but gain a lot. Especially, if you are just out of college then time is on your side to save a nice big next egg. At the minimum, invest the percentage equal to whatever the company matches. This is FREE money you want to take advantage of that investment. If your company offers free one-on-one consultation for managing your 401K, take the free consultation to better understand investments and financial decisions in regards to your different streams of incomes.

For most companies, you can later borrow against 401K money and pay it back with small installments through payroll. You do not want to do this so my advice is to borrow against the

401k plan only for emergencies. Of course, penalties are involved depending on how you withdraw money from this account so check your company policy before making this decision.

From my past experiences, I strongly suggest to never touch your 401K no matter what happens; emergencies, stock market crash or whatever... DO NOT TOUCH IT. You have to make sure you build a good nest egg for later in life because believe you me, you will need it. You will not always be working in corporate America, at some point life changes, retirement happens, accidents happen and you need to be prepared.

9

Create a Cheat Sheet

In my career, I have had many user-ids, passwords, secret questions, e-mail addresses, and projects. Also, in my line of work I have had many systems I need to access in order to perform my job well. To handle all this private information I create an encrypted Cheat Sheet. For projects, I create a Cheat Sheet for each one as well. So I have one Login Cheat Sheet and Project Cheat Sheets per project. The Login Cheat Sheet contains the following:

➢ Every login user-id and password combinations for every system software, hopefully your company has consolidated this to one login,

➢ PC login user-id and password,

➢ Benefits Login user-id and password,

➢ Remote Login user-id and password,

➢ E-mail Login user-id and password

The project Cheat Sheet has

The name of the project,

How to access the system for that project,

Document how the project works,

Run instructions,

Error handling procedure, and

Any special steps of the project I need to remember.

This Cheat Sheet methodology does not do you any justice unless you keep it updated. And by the way, do not write down your password anywhere and definitely do not give it to anyone. Your password is like your SSN and I hope you do know you should not give that to anyone either. This goes back to the first rule – CYA. If anyone has your password, he or she can do anything with your information. So keep it private!

10

Don't Burn Any Bridges

Don't burn a bridge you might have to cross back over one day! Whatever industry you work in, somebody knows somebody that knows you. The longer you work in that industry, the more people you know and the more people who know you. And that my dear is the industry click you have involuntarily been inducted into. You will get to a point in your career where no matter where you work somebody knows you or somebody knows somebody that knows you. That means your reputation will precede you. When it comes time to look for a job it will be your resume, the reputation you have built over the years and who you know that helps you find your next position or promotion. So the moral of this story is don't burn a bridge that you might have to come back across. This means at the current job you are working, your manager and your peers help build your bridge.

You never know which coworker will become your next manager or which company will rehire you because of your previous work ethic. Try your best to be professional, do excellent work and treat coworkers and managers as you want to be treated. This does not mean let someone throw you under the bus. What it means is be professional about any confrontation you have and if you followed the Number 1 Rule-CYA, then you have all the backup you need to defend yourself.

If you have the misfortune of being laid off, be professional; quickly reach out to your network and recruiters to find your next position. There is no need to be upset or give your upper management a piece of your mind. Before you know it that same manager or someone that manager knows will be calling you back because of your reputation. In your career, the only thing you have control of is your reputation made up of your professionalism, work ethic, and personality.

So let me explain further with one of my experiences. Early in my career I worked for this top 100 company. Up until this point it was the easiest and most highly paid contract I had acquired. Three months later I received a two weeks' notice that I would be laid off. I walked around with an attitude against my manager and after a couple of days she called me in her office. I gave her a piece of my mind because there were other contractors who had been hired after me. I did not think it was fair that I was the one laid off and they were not. In hindsight, I had no business speaking to her in my tone but at the time I thought I was soooo justified. I do not know what kind of pressures she was under or what directions given to her by upper management. She did not have any obligations to me, and it was unfair of me to think that she should have. I had not built a significant relationship with her nor had gone out of my way to show her that she could not do without my expertise. So needless to say, I burned that bridge because I thought I was so right.

Nothing is fair in corporate America. I am going to say this again (s l o w l y):

Nothing is fair in corporate America.

It is about who you know and their (the company's) bottom line. You have to make the best decisions for your family. You have to take control over your career and the only person you have control over is ---(wait for it) YOU!!! So it is up to you to build your career, build up your network, beep your own horn, let your work speak volumes and protect your reputation by building your own unique personal brand. Needless to say, future contracts came my way from that same department but for some mysterious reason I could never get an interview in that department... hmmmm I wonder why?

So there you have it! Those are my top ten rules I live by in corporate America and I take them to every job I have had over the last 30 plus years, building my own personal unique brand. I have come by these rules through trials and tribulations as you have read from my real life experiences. I pray for success in your career and I am sure you will develop your own rules as you navigate this corporate environment. So to enhance your unique personal brand start entering your own rules, passwords, cheat sheets in the blank pages that follow. Congratulations in entering into Corporate America and Good luck in your career.

V. M. Singleton.

...and do have a nice day!!!

Managing IT professional teams and projects | Successfully Analyze and Deploy Effective Solutions to Achieve Business Initiatives on time and within budget

ABOUT THE AUTHOR

V. M. Singleton has published and written several literary works. The publishing company VMS Publishings & Productions formed in 2008 published its first book *Mama Down the Bayou Recipes with Shopping Lists*. This Creole cookbook was written by V. M. Singleton and several other authors. She also published and created the cover art for *Barbara Jean Barbara Jean Poetry – A Silhouette of Me* written by B. J. Cleveland.

10 Rules for Minorities Entering Corporate America is her third literary work.

She has worked in Corporate America for over 30 years in the IT industry. Her career expands from AT&T, Nextel, Sprint, Bellsouth Companies, Coca-Cola, MCI, Delta Airlines and many other top 100 companies in America. She has achieved a Bachelor of Science degree and a Masters of Information Systems. Her books are available on Amazon.com, Barnes & Noble and many other websites. Visit her website for more information about her literary works at **www.VMSPublishings.net.**

Rules

_____

_____

_____

_____

_____

_____

_____

_____

_____

_____

_____

_____

_____

_____

_____

_____

_____

_____

_____

_____

_____

_____

_____

_____

Passwords

_____

_____

_____

_____

_____

_____

_____

_____

_____

_____

_____

_____

_____

_____

_____

_____

_____

_____

_____

_____

_____

_____

_____

_____

Cheat Sheet 1

_____

_____

_____

_____

_____

_____

_____

_____

_____

_____

_____

_____

_____

_____

_____

_____

_____

_____

_____

_____

_____

_____

_____

_____

_____

_____

_____

Cheat Sheet 2

_____

_____

_____

_____

_____

_____

_____

_____

_____

_____

_____

_____

_____

_____

_____

_____

_____

_____

_____

_____

_____

_____

_____

_____